BEGINNERS GUIDE TO SHOPIFY

2024

Step-by-step guide to setup a profitable shopify store.

Ella Nelson

Table of contents

INTRODUCTION

In today's digital landscape, the power of e-commerce has transformed the way we shop and sell. E-commerce platforms have become the heartbeat of modern retail, offering entrepreneurs an unprecedented gateway to global markets. Whether you're an aspiring entrepreneur or an established business seeking an online presence, understanding the dynamics of e-commerce platforms is the first step toward success.

What is Shopify?

Shopify is a robust and user-friendly e-commerce platform that empowers businesses of all sizes to create, manage, and scale their online stores with remarkable ease. It serves as a comprehensive toolkit, providing entrepreneurs and merchants with a suite of tools and features to build their digital storefronts and sell products or services to customers worldwide.

At its core, Shopify offers a customizable and intuitive interface, allowing users to set up their online stores without the need for extensive technical expertise. From selecting and customizing themes to managing products, orders, and customer interactions, Shopify streamlines the entire e-commerce process.

The platform caters to various business needs, offering functionalities for inventory management, payment processing, marketing, and analytics. Whether you're a burgeoning startup, an established brand, or an individual entrepreneur, Shopify accommodates diverse industries and scales seamlessly to meet evolving business demands.

With its extensive app ecosystem, Shopify allows users to expand their store's capabilities by integrating numerous third-party apps for added functionalities like accounting, social media marketing, customer support, and more.

In essence, Shopify serves as a one-stop solution, fostering a thriving online presence and enabling businesses to thrive in the competitive landscape of digital commerce.

Benefits of Choosing Shopify

Enter Shopify—a dynamic, user-friendly platform designed to empower businesses of all sizes. With Shopify, the possibilities are boundless. It's more than just an e-commerce platform; it's your launchpad into the digital marketplace. From seamless store setup to powerful marketing tools and robust customer support, Shopify offers a suite of benefits that elevate your online store's potential.

Join us on a journey through the vibrant world of Shopify—a world where setting up and managing your online store is not just hassle-free but an exhilarating experience. Discover how Shopify's intuitive interface, extensive features, and unparalleled support can turn your e-commerce dreams into thriving realities.

Let's embark together on this exciting adventure as we delve into the depths of Shopify, uncovering its wonders and unlocking the doors to your online success.

CHAPTER 1

Setting Up Your Store

Creating Your Shopify Account

Visit the Shopify Website:

- Go to Shopify's official website (www.shopify.com) using a web browser.

Click on "Get Started":

- On the Shopify homepage, locate and click on the "Get Started" button, typically found in the top right corner.

Enter Email and Store Name:

- You'll be prompted to enter your email address and choose a unique name for your store. This name will be part of your store's URL.

Create a Password:

- Set up a secure password for your Shopify account. Ensure it meets the platform's password requirements.

Fill in Personal Details:

- Provide additional information about yourself and your business, including your name, address, and contact information.

Enter Business Details:

- Shopify will ask for details regarding your business, such as your business address, industry, and expected revenue.

Customize Your Store Domain:

- Choose a custom domain name for your store or use the default Shopify-generated domain. This is the web address where customers will access your store.

Complete Payment Setup:

- Set up your preferred payment method to receive payments from customers. Shopify provides various payment gateway options.

Confirm Account Creation:

- Review the information provided, double-checking for accuracy. Then, agree to Shopify's terms of service and privacy policy.

Click "Create Your Store":

- Once all information is entered and verified, click on the button to create your Shopify store.

Access Your Dashboard:

- After creating your account, you'll be directed to your Shopify dashboard. This is where you'll manage all aspects of your store, including adding products, customizing themes, and managing orders.

Congratulations! You've successfully created your Shopify account. From here, you can start setting up your online store and adding products to begin selling. Shopify often offers a trial period, allowing you to explore the platform before choosing a subscription plan.

Navigating the Dashboard

Understanding the Dashboard Layout

Log In to Shopify:

Access the Shopify platform using your login credentials. Upon logging in, you'll land on the main dashboard, the control center of your store.

Dashboard Overview:

The dashboard is divided into sections, offering a comprehensive overview of essential metrics, sales data, and store performance.

Navigation Bar:

Explore the left sidebar navigation. Sections include:

Home: Overview of sales, orders, and store performance.
Orders: Manage orders, view details, and process transactions.
Products: Add, edit, and organize products in your inventory.
Customers: Manage customer profiles, interactions, and contact details.
Analytics: Access reports, sales data, and insights on store performance.
Marketing: Utilize marketing tools, campaigns, and discounts.
Discounts: Create and manage discount codes for promotions.

Apps: Explore and manage installed apps for added functionalities.

Sales Channels: Connect and manage different sales channels like social media or in-person sales.

Settings: Customize store settings, preferences, and configurations.

Dashboard Sections and Functions

Home Section:

Overview of store performance, recent activity, and key statistics like sales trends and customer data.

Orders Section:

View and manage incoming orders, process transactions, and fulfill customer requests. Filter orders by status, date, or customer details.

Products Section:

Add new products, manage inventory, update product details, and organize items into collections or categories.

Customers Section:

Manage customer information, view order history, and communicate with customers directly from the dashboard.

Analytics Section:

Access detailed reports on sales, traffic sources, conversion rates, and customer behavior. Gain insights into store performance and make data-driven decisions.

Marketing and Discounts Sections:

Create marketing campaigns, promotions, and discount codes to drive sales and engage customers.

Apps and Sales Channels:

Explore, install, and manage third-party apps to extend store functionalities. Connect and manage various sales channels to reach a wider audience.

Settings Section:

Customize store preferences, payment options, shipping settings, tax configurations, and other store-related settings.

Customizing the Dashboard

Reports and Widgets:

Customize your dashboard by adding or removing widgets and reports based on your preferences. Tailor the dashboard to display the most relevant metrics for your business.

User Permissions:

Assign specific permissions to staff or team members, controlling their access to different sections of the dashboard based on their roles.

Products Suitable for Selling on Shopify:

Shopify provides a versatile platform for selling a broad range of products and services, empowering entrepreneurs to showcase their offerings and reach a global audience. Here's a brief overview of what one can sell on Shopify:

Physical Products:

Clothing and fashion accessories
Electronics and gadgets
Home and kitchen appliances
Health and beauty products
Sports equipment and outdoor gear

Digital Products:

E-books, courses, and educational content
Software, apps, and digital downloads
Artwork, graphic design, and digital assets
Subscriptions and memberships

Handcrafted and Unique Items:

Handmade crafts, jewelry, and art pieces
Vintage or antique collectibles
Customized or personalized items

Dropshipping Products:

Niche-specific items sourced from suppliers

Trending or popular products in the market

Services and Consultations:

Online coaching or consulting services
Freelance services (writing, design, etc.)
Event planning and specialized services

Adding and Managing Products

Successfully adding and managing products on Shopify involves meticulous attention to detail, effective organization, and optimization for customer engagement. The platform accommodates a wide range of products, from physical goods to digital downloads, catering to various industries and business models.

Adding Products:

Access the Products Section:

From your Shopify dashboard, navigate to the 'Products' section.
Click on 'Add product' to start adding a new item to your inventory.

Enter Product Details:

Input the product's title, description, and price. Be descriptive and engaging to entice potential customers.
Add high-quality images that showcase the product from multiple angles.

Organize Product Data:

Categorize products into collections or categories to enhance navigation.

Set product variants (sizes, colors) and manage inventory for each variant separately.

SEO Optimization:

Optimize product descriptions, titles, and tags with relevant keywords for improved search engine visibility.

Customize Product Settings:

Adjust product visibility, availability, and publish dates as needed.
Enable product reviews and ratings to build credibility and trust.

Managing Products:

Product Editing:

Update existing product details, modify prices, descriptions, or images whenever necessary.

Inventory Management:

Track and manage inventory levels, set low stock alerts, and restock products in a timely manner.

Use SKU numbers to uniquely identify products for efficient inventory tracking.

Bulk Editing and Imports:

Use bulk editing tools or import/export functionalities to update multiple products simultaneously.

Product Variants and Options:

Add multiple variants of a product (sizes, colors) and manage inventory separately for each variant.

Offer customizable options for products to allow customers to personalize purchases.

CHAPTER 2

Store Design and Customization

Choosing and Customizing Themes

Selecting the right theme and customizing it effectively plays a pivotal role in shaping the visual appeal and functionality of your Shopify store. Here's a step-by-step guide:

Choosing a Theme:

Explore the Theme Store:
Navigate to the Shopify Theme Store from your dashboard. Browse through a diverse range of free and paid themes.

Consider Your Brand and Niche:
Choose a theme that aligns with your brand identity, target audience, and the nature of your products or services.
Look for themes that offer features suitable for your industry and business needs.

Evaluate Features and Customizability:
Review theme demos and explore their features. Consider aspects like mobile responsiveness, navigation styles, product display, and ease of customization.
Prioritize themes with intuitive interfaces and flexible customization options.

Read Reviews and Ratings:
Check reviews and ratings provided by other users to gauge the theme's performance, support, and overall satisfaction.

Preview and Install:
Preview shortlisted themes on your store to visualize how they'll look and function.
Once decided, install the chosen theme and make it active on your Shopify store.

Customizing the Theme:

Access Theme Settings:
From the Shopify dashboard, navigate to 'Online Store' > 'Themes.' Click 'Customize' on the installed theme.

Basic Customizations:
Customize basic settings like fonts, colors, and typography to align with your brand identity.
Adjust header and footer styles, background colors, and button designs for a cohesive look.

Homepage Layout and Sections:
Modify the homepage layout using customizable sections. Add or rearrange sections for featured products, banners, testimonials, etc.
Customize individual sections to showcase content and visuals that resonate with your audience.

Product Pages and Navigation:
Tailor product page layouts, optimize product descriptions, and enhance image galleries for a visually appealing and informative experience.
Refine navigation menus for ease of use, ensuring intuitive pathways for customers to explore your store.

Mobile Responsiveness:
Optimize your theme for mobile devices. Ensure a seamless and user-friendly experience across various screen sizes.

App Integrations and Advanced Features:
Explore and integrate third-party apps for enhanced functionality, such as social media integrations, email marketing tools, or advanced SEO features.

Preview and Publish:
Preview your customized theme to ensure it aligns with your vision and functions seamlessly.
Once satisfied, save changes and publish the customized theme to make it live on your Shopify store.

Creating Compelling Product Pages

By implementing these strategies, you can create compelling product pages on Shopify that effectively showcase your products, engage customers, and drive conversions. Each element should work cohesively to provide valuable information, instill confidence, and guide customers towards making a purchase decision.

Optimizing Product Information:

Engaging Product Titles:

Craft descriptive and concise titles that capture the essence of the product.

Include keywords relevant to the product and its category for improved SEO.

Detailed Descriptions:

Write engaging and informative product descriptions that highlight features, benefits, and unique selling points.

Use persuasive language, storytelling, and bullet points to make the information easily digestible.

Visual Appeal with High-Quality Images:

Showcase products with high-resolution images from multiple angles.

Use zoom-in features and image galleries to allow customers to view product details closely.

Video Demonstrations (if applicable):

Incorporate product demonstration videos to showcase usage, functionality, or unique features.

Videos can enhance customer understanding and increase engagement.

Enhancing User Experience:

Clear Call-to-Action (CTA):

Use clear and compelling CTAs such as "Add to Cart," "Buy Now," or "Learn More."
Ensure the CTA buttons stand out and are easily accessible on the page.

Size Guides and Measurement Charts:

Provide size guides or measurement charts for apparel, shoes, or products requiring size considerations.
Assist customers in making informed purchase decisions, reducing returns.

Customer Reviews and Testimonials:

Display customer reviews and testimonials to build trust and credibility.
Encourage customers to leave reviews by offering incentives or follow-up emails.

Product Variants and Options:

Clearly display product variants (sizes, colors) with dropdown menus or swatches for easy selection.
Enable customization options if applicable, allowing customers to personalize their purchases.

SEO Optimization:

Keyword-Rich Content:
Incorporate relevant keywords in product descriptions, titles, and meta tags for better search engine visibility.
Use long-tail keywords that align with customer search queries.

Structured Data and Schema Markup:
Implement structured data to provide search engines with additional product information.
Utilize schema markup for rich snippets in search results, enhancing visibility.

Mobile Optimization:

Responsive Design:
Ensure product pages are optimized for mobile devices with responsive design and fast loading times.
Maintain a user-friendly layout and easy navigation on smaller screens.

Mobile-Friendly Visuals:
Use images and videos optimized for mobile viewing without compromising quality.

Cross-Selling and Upselling:

Related Products and Bundles:
Recommend related or complementary products on the product page to encourage additional purchases.

Create product bundles or kits to offer value and increase average order value.

Limited-Time Offers or Discounts:
Highlight special offers, discounts, or limited-time promotions to entice customers to make a purchase.

Mobile Optimization

Mobile devices account for a significant portion of online traffic and purchases. Mobile optimization on Shopify is a continual process that focuses on providing a seamless and engaging experience for users accessing your store via mobile devices. It caters to this growing segment of users.

Responsive design ensures that your store adapts to various screen sizes and resolutions, providing an optimal viewing experience on smartphones and tablets.

Mobile users expect quick loading times. Optimize images, minimize scripts, and leverage browser caching to enhance site speed on mobile devices.

Steps for Mobile Optimization

Mobile-First Design Approach:
Adopt a mobile-first approach in designing your Shopify store. Ensure that the layout, navigation, and content are intuitive and easily accessible on mobile devices.

Choose a Mobile-Friendly Theme:
Select a Shopify theme that is mobile-responsive by default. Ensure it retains visual appeal and functionality across different devices.

Streamlined Navigation:
Simplify navigation menus and buttons for easy access on smaller screens. Use collapsible menus or hamburger icons for a clutter-free experience.

Optimize Visual Elements:
Compress images without compromising quality to reduce load times on mobile devices.
Use mobile-optimized videos and graphics to enhance engagement without consuming excessive bandwidth.

Responsive Typography:
Ensure text is legible and easy to read on mobile screens. Use fonts and font sizes that are comfortable for mobile users without requiring zooming.

Mobile-Specific CTAs:
Place clear and prominent call-to-action (CTA) buttons that are easily clickable on mobile screens. Ensure they stand out and prompt action.

Touch-Friendly Interface:
Ensure elements like buttons, links, and forms are adequately spaced and large enough to be tapped easily on touchscreens.

Optimized Checkout Process:
Simplify the checkout process for mobile users. Minimize form fields, offer guest checkout options, and provide secure payment methods optimized for mobile devices.

Testing and Analysis

Mobile-Friendly Test:
Use Google's Mobile-Friendly Test or Shopify's built-in tools to assess your store's mobile compatibility and identify areas for improvement.

Performance Monitoring:
Continuously monitor site performance using tools like Google PageSpeed Insights or Shopify's analytics to identify and address any mobile-specific performance issues.

User Experience Analysis:
Gather feedback from users, conduct usability tests, and analyze user behavior on mobile devices to refine and improve the mobile experience.

App Integration for Enhanced Mobile Experience

Shopify Mobile App:
Leverage Shopify's mobile app to manage your store, track sales, and engage with customers on the go.

Third-Party Integrations:

Explore and integrate third-party apps that offer mobile-specific functionalities like push notifications, live chat support, or mobile marketing tools.

CHAPTER 3

Managing Orders and Customers

Order Processing and Fulfillment

Order Processing:

Viewing Orders:

Access the 'Orders' section in your Shopify dashboard to view and manage incoming orders.
Sort orders by status, date, or customer details for efficient handling.

Order Status Management:

Manage order statuses (e.g., pending, processing, fulfilled) to track order progress.
Use Shopify's order tags or custom order statuses for better organization.

Order Editing and Modifications:

Make necessary changes to orders before fulfillment, such as updating shipping addresses or adding/removing items.
Notify customers about modifications through order status updates or personalized communication.

Automated Order Notifications:

Set up automated order confirmation emails and shipping notifications to keep customers informed about their purchase and shipment status.

Fulfillment Process:

Fulfillment Options:

Fulfill orders directly within Shopify's dashboard or integrate with third-party fulfillment services.
Choose from options like self-fulfillment, dropshipping, or outsourced fulfillment centers based on your business model.

Generating Shipping Labels:

Create shipping labels directly through Shopify, or integrate with shipping carriers to generate labels.
Print labels and packing slips for accurate order fulfillment.

Multi-Location Inventory Management:

Manage inventory across multiple locations or warehouses using Shopify's inventory tools.
Utilize location-based fulfillment for efficient order processing and reduced shipping times.

Bulk Order Fulfillment:

Streamline the fulfillment process by fulfilling multiple orders in bulk, saving time and effort.
Use batch order processing for smoother operations, especially during peak periods.

Tracking and Delivery Confirmation:

Provide tracking numbers to customers for package visibility.
Update order statuses and provide delivery confirmations once orders are successfully delivered.

Backorder and Preorder Management:

Handle backorders or preorder items by setting clear expectations with customers about delivery timelines.
Communicate proactively about any delays or updates regarding these orders.

Returns and Refunds:

Return Management:

Establish clear return policies and procedures for customers.
Manage returns efficiently by processing refund requests and issuing return labels if applicable.

Refund Processing:

Process refunds directly from Shopify's dashboard for seamless and transparent transactions.
Monitor return patterns to identify product issues or areas for improvement.

Integration and Analytics:

Integration with Apps and Tools:

Integrate with shipping apps, inventory management tools, or third-party logistics providers to streamline the fulfillment process.
Automate tasks and improve efficiency with specialized apps for order processing and fulfillment.

Analytics and Reporting:

Analyze fulfillment metrics and reports within Shopify to optimize processes and identify bottlenecks.
Monitor fulfillment speed, accuracy, and customer satisfaction to continuously improve operations.

Customer Management

Customer management involves the strategies, practices, and tools used by businesses to interact with, retain, and build relationships with their customers throughout their lifecycle.
It encompasses various aspects of customer interaction and satisfaction, aiming to meet their needs, enhance their

experience, and foster loyalty.Effective customer management focuses on building strong relationships, understanding customer needs, and consistently delivering value. It's a continuous process that prioritizes customer satisfaction and retention, ultimately contributing to business growth and success. Here are key components to note on customer management:

Customer Relationship Management (CRM):

Utilizing CRM systems to gather and manage customer data, including contact details, purchase history, preferences, and interactions. This information helps in personalized communication and targeted marketing efforts.

Customer Engagement:

Engaging customers through various channels like email, social media, live chat, and phone calls. Providing valuable content, responding promptly to inquiries, and seeking feedback enhances engagement.

Customer Support and Service:

Providing excellent customer service by addressing inquiries, concerns, and complaints effectively and efficiently. Offering multiple support channels and ensuring a positive resolution of issues is crucial.

Personalization and Customization:

Tailoring products, services, and communication based on individual customer preferences and behaviors. Personalization creates a more meaningful and relevant customer experience.

Feedback and Surveys:

Collecting feedback through surveys, reviews, and follow-ups to understand customer satisfaction, preferences, and areas for improvement. Using this feedback to refine products/services.

Retention and Loyalty Programs:

Implementing loyalty programs, rewards, and incentives to encourage repeat purchases and foster long-term relationships. Acknowledging and rewarding loyal customers is key.

Data Analysis and Insights:

Analyzing customer data to gain insights into buying patterns, trends, and behaviors. This information helps in predicting customer needs and tailoring marketing strategies.

Customer Journey Mapping:

Mapping out the customer journey from the initial interaction to post-purchase experiences. Understanding touchpoints helps in optimizing interactions and resolving pain points.

Cross-selling and Upselling:

Identifying opportunities to recommend complementary products or upgrades based on customer needs or past purchases. This can increase the average order value.

Adapting to Customer Needs:

Flexibility in adapting products/services based on changing customer preferences, market trends, or feedback received, ensuring relevance.

Handling Returns and Refunds

Handling returns and refunds is a critical aspect of customer service and maintaining positive relationships with customers. To manage returns and refunds effectively:

Establish a transparent and easily accessible return policy outlining the conditions, timeframes, and procedures for returns and refunds. Display it prominently on your website and during the purchasing process. Simplify the return process by providing clear instructions and easy-to-use return forms or portals. Include prepaid return labels for convenience.

Respond swiftly to return requests or inquiries. Acknowledge receipt of return requests and provide customers with clear timelines for processing their returns or refunds. Upon receiving returned items, promptly inspect them to ensure they meet the return conditions specified in your policy (e.g., unused, undamaged, in original packaging).

Process refunds promptly once returns are approved. Clearly communicate the refund amount and expected timelines for the funds to reflect in the customer's account. Adopt a customer-first approach when handling returns. Be empathetic, understanding, and accommodating to customers' concerns, even if the return doesn't meet the ideal conditions.

Analyze return data to identify patterns or common issues leading to returns. Use this information to improve product descriptions, packaging, or overall quality. Encourage customers to provide feedback when initiating a return. This insight can help address recurring issues and improve customer satisfaction.

Utilize automation tools or software to streamline return authorizations, generate return labels, and track return statuses. This can expedite the process and reduce manual workload. Regularly review and refine your return policies and procedures based on customer feedback and return trends. Aim to make the process more customer-friendly and efficient.

Remember, a smooth return and refund experience can positively impact customer loyalty and satisfaction, even if the initial purchase didn't work out. By prioritizing customer needs and ensuring a hassle-free return process, businesses can build trust and credibility with their customer base.

CHAPTER 4

Marketing Strategies

Marketing strategies on Shopify involve the use of various techniques and approaches to promote products or services, attract potential customers, and drive sales on the platform. Here are several marketing strategies commonly employed on Shopify, Implementing a combination of these marketing strategies tailored to your brand, target audience, and products can significantly boost visibility, engagement, and sales on the Shopify platform. It's crucial to analyze and refine these strategies based on data and customer feedback for continued success.

Content Marketing:

Blogging: Creating engaging and informative blog content related to your products or industry can attract organic traffic, improve SEO, and establish your brand as an authority.
Visual Content: Using visually appealing content like images, infographics, and videos to showcase products and convey brand messages effectively.

Search Engine Optimization (SEO):

Optimizing product pages, descriptions, and website content with relevant keywords and metadata to improve search engine rankings and visibility.

Email Marketing:

Building an email list and sending targeted and personalized emails to subscribers about promotions, new products, or exclusive offers. Utilizing automated email sequences for abandoned carts or follow-ups.

Social Media Marketing:

Leveraging social media platforms to reach and engage with a wider audience. Running targeted ads, sharing product updates, and interacting with customers on platforms like Facebook, Instagram, Twitter, and Pinterest.

Influencer Marketing:

Collaborating with influencers or micro-influencers who align with your brand to promote products or services to their audience. This can increase brand visibility and credibility.

Paid Advertising:

Using paid advertising channels like Google Ads, Facebook Ads, or Instagram Ads to target specific demographics and retarget website visitors, driving traffic and conversions.

Referral Programs:

Encouraging existing customers to refer friends or family by offering incentives or discounts for successful referrals. This helps in acquiring new customers through word-of-mouth marketing.

Discounts and Promotions:

Offering time-limited discounts, coupon codes, or special promotions to entice potential customers and encourage purchases.

Customer Retention Strategies:

Implementing strategies like loyalty programs, personalized recommendations, or exclusive offers for returning customers to encourage repeat purchases and enhance customer lifetime value.

Collaborations and Partnerships:

Collaborating with complementary brands or businesses for cross-promotions, joint campaigns, or co-marketing efforts, expanding the customer base and reaching new audiences.

Designing Marketing Plans

By integrating these detailed design-focused strategies into your Shopify marketing plan, you can create a visually compelling and user-centric shopping experience, fostering customer engagement and driving conversions. Design plays an important role in enhancing brand perception and building trust, ultimately contributing to the success of your Shopify store.

1. Visual Branding and Identity:

Establish a consistent visual identity that reflects your brand. Define brand colors, typography, logo, and overall design elements across your Shopify store, ensuring coherence and recognition.

2. Website Design and User Experience (UX):

Craft an intuitive and visually appealing website design. Ensure ease of navigation, clear product categorization, high-quality imagery, and persuasive call-to-action buttons to enhance user experience and encourage conversions.

3. Product Presentation and Visual Merchandising:

Optimize product presentation by using high-resolution images, engaging videos, and 360-degree views where applicable. Curate visually appealing collections, highlight bestsellers, and use lifestyle imagery to showcase products effectively.

4. Mobile Responsiveness and Adaptability:

Prioritize mobile responsiveness in design to cater to the growing number of mobile users. Ensure that your Shopify store functions seamlessly across various devices and screen sizes.

5. Landing Page and Conversion Optimization:

Design persuasive landing pages tailored to specific campaigns or product launches. Implement A/B testing to refine landing page design elements, such as headlines, visuals, and CTAs, for optimal conversions.

6. Visual Content Creation:
Invest in visually engaging content creation, including product photography, graphics, infographics, and videos. Visual content plays a pivotal role in attracting and retaining customers' attention.

7. Brand Storytelling through Design:
Leverage design elements to narrate your brand's story and values effectively. Use visuals and graphics to communicate brand messages, ethos, and the value proposition to resonate with your audience.

8. User Interface (UI) and Customer Journey Mapping:
Focus on user interface design to create a seamless and intuitive shopping experience. Map out the customer journey, ensuring a visually guided path from browsing to checkout, reducing friction points.

9. Visual Marketing Collaterals:
Create visually appealing marketing collateral such as banners, ads, social media graphics, and email templates. Consistent and eye-catching visuals can reinforce brand recall and engagement.

10. Data-Driven Design Optimization:
Utilize analytics tools to track user behavior, engagement metrics, and conversion rates. Use this data to optimize design elements,

refine user experience, and improve overall performance continually.

11. Collaboration with Design Professionals:
Consider collaborating with experienced designers or agencies to leverage their expertise in creating captivating designs, ensuring a polished and professional appearance for your brand.

12. Iterative Improvements and Adaptation:
Continuously iterate and refine design elements based on user feedback, industry trends, and performance metrics. Adapt to evolving consumer preferences and market changes to stay relevant.

Social Media Integration and SEO Techniques for Visibility

Integrating social media and implementing effective SEO techniques are pivotal strategies for enhancing visibility and driving traffic to your Shopify store. Here's a detailed breakdown of both:

Social Media Integration

Cross-platform Presence: Establish a strong presence on relevant social media platforms where your target audience is active. This may include platforms like Facebook, Instagram, Twitter, Pinterest, LinkedIn, or TikTok.

Consistent Branding: Maintain consistency in branding across all social media channels. Use cohesive profile images, cover photos, and bios that reflect your brand identity.

Engaging Content: Create diverse and engaging content tailored to each platform. Share product showcases, behind-the-scenes glimpses, user-generated content, polls, stories, and interactive posts to engage your audience.

Community Engagement: Foster engagement by responding to comments, messages, and mentions promptly. Encourage user-generated content, run contests, and engage in conversations to build a loyal community around your brand.

Paid Advertising: Utilize paid advertising options available on social media platforms to reach a wider audience. Target specific demographics, retarget website visitors, and create compelling ad creatives to drive traffic to your Shopify store.

SEO Techniques for Visibility

Keyword Research: Conduct thorough keyword research to identify relevant and high-volume search terms related to your products or industry. Use tools like Google Keyword Planner or SEMrush to find valuable keywords.

Optimized Product Pages: Optimize product titles, descriptions, and meta tags with targeted keywords. Ensure descriptions are unique, informative, and include relevant keywords while avoiding keyword stuffing.

Site Structure and Navigation: Ensure a clear and logical site structure for easy navigation. Use breadcrumbs, internal linking, and a sitemap to enhance user experience and search engine crawling.

High-Quality Content: Produce high-quality, valuable content such as blogs, guides, or videos relevant to your niche. Create content that addresses user queries, provides solutions, or offers valuable insights, contributing to higher search engine rankings.

Mobile Optimization: Optimize your Shopify store for mobile devices. With a significant portion of users accessing sites through mobile, a responsive and mobile-friendly design is crucial for SEO rankings.

Page Load Speed: Improve site loading speed by optimizing images, leveraging browser caching, and using content delivery networks (CDNs). Faster loading times positively impact user experience and SEO rankings.

Backlink Building: Acquire high-quality backlinks from authoritative and relevant websites. Collaborate with influencers, guest post on reputable sites, or engage in partnerships to gain quality backlinks, boosting your site's authority.

Regular Monitoring and Analysis: Use tools like Google Analytics and Google Search Console to monitor site performance, track traffic, identify keywords driving traffic, and analyze user behavior. Adjust strategies based on data insights to optimize performance continually.

CHAPTER 5

Utilizing Shopify Apps

Shopify's App Store is a treasure trove of tools and solutions designed to enhance various facets of your e-commerce venture. By exploring, installing, and managing apps strategically, businesses can leverage these powerful tools to streamline operations, optimize marketing efforts, improve customer experiences, and drive sustainable growth. Regularly reassess and refine your app ecosystem to ensure it aligns with your business objectives and evolves with your company's needs.

Exploring App Store Options

Shopify's App Store offers a vast array of applications catering to different business needs. Start by exploring categories such as Marketing, Sales, Customer Service, Inventory Management, and more. Use filters to narrow down options based on features, ratings, reviews, and compatibility with your Shopify store's requirements. Look for apps with robust functionalities, positive reviews, and a track record of delivering value to similar businesses.

Installing and Managing Apps:

Once you've identified suitable apps, installing them onto your Shopify store is straightforward. Simply navigate to the Shopify App Store, select the desired app, and click 'Add app.' Follow the prompts to authorize the app's access to your store. After installation, manage your apps from the Shopify admin panel. Access the 'Apps' section to configure settings, access support, or uninstall apps if they don't meet your needs. Regularly review installed apps to ensure they align with your evolving business goals.

Leveraging Apps for Growth:

Shopify apps play a pivotal role in business growth, offering tools and functionalities to streamline operations, enhance customer experiences, and boost sales. Here are key areas where apps can drive growth:

1. Marketing and Sales:
Leverage marketing apps for email campaigns, social media integration, SEO optimization, and abandoned cart recovery. Sales-centric apps can assist in upselling, cross-selling, discount management, and creating compelling product offers.

2. Customer Service and Experience:
Utilize customer service apps for live chat, ticket management, and customer feedback. Implement customer loyalty programs, reviews, and personalized recommendations to enhance customer experience and retention.

3. Inventory and Order Management:

Apps for inventory management, order fulfillment, and shipping optimization streamline backend operations. Automated inventory tracking, reorder alerts, and efficient shipping solutions help maintain smooth operations.

4. Analytics and Reporting:

Install analytics apps to gain insights into sales trends, customer behavior, and website performance. Analyze data to make informed decisions and refine marketing strategies for better results.

5. Accounting and Finance:

Opt for accounting apps that seamlessly integrate with Shopify for streamlined financial management, bookkeeping, and tax calculations, ensuring accurate financial records and compliance.

6. Scalability and Customization:

As your business grows, explore apps that offer scalability and customization options. Look for apps that adapt to changing needs, offer scalability without sacrificing performance, and allow customization to align with your brand's uniqueness.

7. Automation and Efficiency:

Apps that automate repetitive tasks, streamline workflows, and improve operational efficiency are invaluable. They save time, reduce errors, and allow you to focus on strategic aspects of your business.

CHAPTER 6

Payment, Security, and Checkout on Shopify

Payment, Security, and Checkout processes in a Shopify store are pivotal components influencing customer trust, satisfaction, and overall business success. By setting up secure payment gateways, prioritizing store security, and optimizing the checkout experience, businesses can instill confidence in customers, reduce cart abandonment rates, and foster long-term relationships. Regularly assess and update security measures, payment options, and checkout processes to adapt to evolving industry standards and customer expectations.

Setting Up Payment Gateways

Shopify offers various payment gateway options allowing customers to make secure transactions. Begin by accessing your Shopify admin panel and navigating to 'Settings' > 'Payment Providers.' Here, you can choose from Shopify Payments, third-party providers like PayPal, Stripe, or other regional options. Configure your preferred payment gateways by entering necessary details and ensuring they align with your business location, currency, and customer preferences. Offering multiple payment options enhances customer convenience and reduces cart abandonment rates.

Securing Your Store

Ensuring robust security measures within your Shopify store is paramount to safeguard sensitive customer data and build trust. Start by using HTTPS encryption, which Shopify provides by default, ensuring secure data transmission. Regularly update your store's software, including apps and themes, to patch vulnerabilities. Implement strong password policies, enable two-factor authentication, and limit staff access to sensitive data. Additionally, consider obtaining an SSL (Secure Sockets Layer) Certificate and comply with PCI DSS(Payment Card Industry Data Security Standards) to secure payment information.

Optimizing Checkout Experience

A smooth and intuitive checkout process is crucial for reducing cart abandonment rates and improving customer satisfaction. Customize your checkout settings in the Shopify admin panel to streamline the process. Enable guest checkout options, minimize form fields, and provide clear instructions to reduce friction. Implement autofill features, offer multiple payment methods, and display shipping costs upfront to avoid surprises at checkout. Test your checkout process regularly, seeking feedback from users, and use analytics to identify and address bottlenecks or barriers hindering the checkout flow.

Payment Gateway Optimization

Selecting the right payment gateways is vital. Evaluate transaction fees, processing times, and geographic coverage to choose gateways that suit your business and customer needs. Consider offering various payment options such as credit/debit cards, digital wallets, or local payment methods to cater to diverse customer preferences. Additionally, optimize checkout for mobile devices, ensuring a seamless experience across different devices and screen sizes.

Fraud Prevention and Risk Management:

Implement fraud prevention tools and strategies to protect your store and customers from fraudulent activities. Utilize fraud detection apps, address verification systems, and risk assessment tools provided by payment gateways. Set up fraud analysis in your Shopify store to identify suspicious transactions and set thresholds for order reviews. Train your staff to recognize potential fraud indicators and implement manual verification steps when necessary.

Customer Data Protection:

Maintain strict compliance with data protection regulations like GDPR (General Data Protection Regulation), CCPA (California Consumer Privacy Act), or other regional laws governing customer data. Clearly communicate your privacy policy, ensure customer consent for data collection, and use secure data storage methods. Regularly audit your store's data handling processes and review third-party app permissions to minimize data exposure.

CHAPTER 7

Analytics and Performance

Understanding Shopify Analytics:

Shopify provides a range of analytics tools and insights to help merchants understand their store performance and customer behavior. Access your Shopify admin panel and navigate to the 'Analytics' section. Here, you'll find comprehensive data on sales, traffic sources, conversion rates, customer behavior, and more. Utilize features like overview dashboards, real-time reports, and data breakdowns to gain valuable insights into your store's performance.

Monitoring Sales Metrics:

Key sales metrics provide critical insights into your store's performance and can guide decision-making. Monitor metrics such as total sales, average order value, conversion rates, and sales by product or category. Track trends over time, analyze seasonal variations, and identify top-performing products or marketing campaigns. Understanding these metrics allows for better sales forecasting, inventory management, and targeted marketing efforts.

Using Reports for Improvement:

Shopify's reporting tools offer customizable and detailed reports that help identify strengths, weaknesses, and growth opportunities. Use reports to analyze customer demographics, referral sources, abandoned carts, and purchase patterns. Leverage this information to refine marketing strategies, improve user experience, and optimize product offerings. Identify areas for improvement, such as checkout funnel optimization, and use A/B testing to measure the impact of changes.

Conversion Funnel Analysis:

Analyze the conversion funnel to understand the customer journey from browsing to purchase. Identify potential drop-off points in the funnel, such as high cart abandonment rates or lengthy checkout processes. Optimize each stage of the funnel by streamlining processes, improving website navigation, and providing clear calls-to-action to enhance conversion rates.

Customer Lifetime Value (CLV):

Understanding the CLV helps in assessing the long-term value of a customer to your business. Calculate the CLV by analyzing repeat purchases, average order frequency, and customer retention rates. Focus on strategies to increase CLV, such as personalized marketing, loyalty programs, and excellent customer service to maximize revenue from each customer.

Data-Driven Decision Making:

Utilize Shopify's analytics and reporting capabilities to make informed, data-driven decisions. Base marketing campaigns, inventory planning, and website optimizations on insights gleaned from analytics. Continuously monitor and iterate strategies based on data trends to drive continuous improvement and maximize business growth.

CHAPTER 8

Scaling Your Business

Scalability involves a combination of operational efficiency, strategic planning, technology adoption, and a customer-centric approach to support the evolving needs of a growing business.

By systematically implementing these strategies, businesses on Shopify can scale operations effectively, expand their customer base, increase revenue, and achieve sustainable growth.

1. Optimize Operations for Growth:

Streamline workflows and operational processes to handle increased demand efficiently. Automate repetitive tasks, enhance inventory management, and optimize fulfillment and shipping processes to accommodate higher order volumes.

2. Expand Product Offerings:

Diversify your product range to attract a broader customer base. Conduct market research to identify complementary or trending products that align with your brand. Introduce new product lines, variations, or exclusive offerings to cater to diverse customer needs.

3. Enhance Marketing Strategies:

Scale up marketing efforts to reach a wider audience. Invest in targeted advertising campaigns, expand social media presence, and collaborate with influencers or affiliates to increase brand visibility. Focus on customer retention strategies alongside acquisition to nurture long-term relationships.

4. Upgrade Technology and Infrastructure:

Assess your technological infrastructure and upgrade systems to support increased traffic and sales. Ensure your website is scalable, mobile-optimized, and equipped to handle higher volumes without compromising performance.

5. Optimize Customer Service and Support:

Scale your customer service capabilities to maintain high-quality support as your business grows. Implement chatbots, expand support channels, and train additional staff to handle increased inquiries promptly and effectively.

6. Explore International Markets:

Consider expanding into international markets to tap into new customer segments. Adapt marketing strategies, localize content, and comply with regional regulations to successfully enter new markets and cater to diverse audiences.

7. Collaborate and Partner:

Form partnerships with complementary businesses or influencers to leverage their audiences and expand your reach. Collaborate with suppliers or manufacturers to negotiate better terms or introduce exclusive products.

8. Analyze Data for Scalability:

Continuously analyze data and key performance indicators (KPIs) to identify growth opportunities and potential bottlenecks. Use insights from analytics to make informed decisions and optimize strategies for scalability.

9. Invest in Scalable Solutions:
Implement scalable solutions and technologies that grow with your business. Consider cloud-based services, scalable e-commerce platforms, and flexible software solutions that adapt to changing business needs.

10. Financial Planning and Investment:
Plan and allocate resources strategically to support growth initiatives. Secure funding, if necessary, and invest in areas that offer the most significant potential for scalability while maintaining financial stability.

11. Continual Optimization and Adaptation:
Embrace a culture of continual optimization and adaptation. Test and iterate strategies, stay abreast of industry trends, and be agile in responding to market changes to remain competitive.

CHAPTER 9

Customer Support and Service

Customer support and service are vital components of a successful Shopify business, contributing significantly to customer satisfaction, retention, and brand reputation.

Offer support across multiple channels such as live chat, email, phone, and social media platforms. Provide a seamless experience for customers to reach out and receive assistance through their preferred channel.

Aim for prompt responses to customer inquiries. Establish service level agreements (SLAs) for response times and ensure your support team is equipped to handle queries efficiently.

Create a comprehensive knowledge base or FAQ section on your website to address common queries. Provide self-service options and instructional guides to empower customers to find solutions independently.

Provide personalized support by addressing customers by their names and tailoring solutions to their specific needs. Use customer data to anticipate their requirements and offer personalized recommendations.

Consider offering round-the-clock support, especially for critical issues or inquiries. If not feasible, clearly communicate your support hours and response times to manage customer expectations.

Train support staff to communicate empathetically and actively listen to customer concerns. Empathy and understanding go a long way in resolving issues and building rapport with customers.

Gather feedback from customers regularly to gauge satisfaction levels and identify areas for improvement. Use surveys, feedback forms, or review platforms to collect and analyze customer feedback.

Strive for first-contact resolution of issues whenever possible. Equip support teams with the necessary tools and authority to resolve issues promptly, minimizing the need for multiple interactions.

Invest in ongoing training programs for support staff to enhance product knowledge, communication skills, and problem-solving abilities. Stay updated with industry trends and best practices.

Anticipate potential issues or concerns by monitoring trends or patterns in customer queries. Initiate proactive communication, such as informing customers about service disruptions or providing updates on orders.

Utilize customer service metrics like Net Promoter Score (NPS), customer satisfaction (CSAT), and resolution times to measure performance. Use insights to refine support strategies continually.

Establish clear escalation paths for complex or unresolved issues. Ensure there's a system in place for escalating concerns to higher tiers of support or management when necessary.

NOTES